"Curve is a word," writes Kat
language tuned to its best, woı
language provides us imbues the poems again and again, but not just
for words' own sake—we are swept into life, its travails, its happiness,
its ordinary walks in woods and fields. Daughter, wife, mother,
teacher—Reavey explores her roles. As in the best poems, the everyday
becomes ontological—we are allowed to explore who and why we are.
Grasses and berries speak to time and distance. Warmth finds its way
back home. The poems for Reavey's mother, especially moving, show
the path grief takes year after year, losing us and finding us. At last,
this remarkable book—what a cause for celebration.
—Alice Derry, author of *Asking*

The poems in Kate Reavey's *Curve* tenderly follow the contours of a
fully embodied life—the lush hums of desire, the hard swerves of grief.
Her steadfast attention to the way light defines the places and people
she loves evokes the solace of timeless wonder.
—H.K. Hummel, author of *Lessons in Breathing Underwater*

Kate Reavey's clear and welcoming poems speak honestly and passion-
ately of her life as a woman: daughter and mother, wife, and teacher.
Her poems are intimate with the Earth and its seasons and creatures:
bees, birds, and berries. But these poems also plunge into deep pools
of grief and loss—and surface aptly into the transformative power of
the present. Kate reminds me of the supremacy of love in a world of
impermanence, that language is "the only way to bring the weapons
down," and that the astonishing newness of the world awaits only our
attention.
—Tim McNulty, author of *Ascendance*

Brimming with life, Kate Reavey's luminous poems grow out of a love
of family, of the world of nature, and the carrying power of language.
With an ear fine-tuned to prompts from the universe, she alerts us to
the contradictions and uncertainties of living, without diminishing the
love that steadies and enables us. She knows, too, how to release the
hidden music in language—the rhyming and chiming of words, the
suppleness of lines, syllables with their heft and curl—bringing us
closer to the body of the world, to "the buzz and shimmer" of life:
"we write. . . to hear the tunes of blackbirds and fiddles / to hear the
click of the clogs on a young girl's feet."
—Charlotte Gould Warren, author of *Dangerous Bodies*

CURVE

CURVE

POEMS BY
KATE REAVEY

Empty Bowl
Chimacum, Washington

Since 1976, Empty Bowl Press has published literary anthologies, collections of poetry, and Chinese translations. The press promotes the work of writers and artists who share our founding purpose and fundamental theme: literature and responsibility in support of human communities and wild places.

Library of Congress Control Number: 2022945182
ISBN 978-1-73704-088-0

Cover art: Rebecca Wild, *Kelp Bouquet*. Acrylics, graphite, and pastel on wood panel, 20 inches × 20 inches. The cover image was inspired by the poem "Morse Creek Turning."

Cover design: Lauren Grosskopf

EMPTY BOWL
2232 West Valley Road
Chimacum, Washington 98325

www.emptybowl.org
editor@emptybowl.org

for Tom, Maeve, and Liam (sometimes known as Fion)

Contents

Acknowledgments

Crosscurrents 2020: "Almost Talking" and "March 11"

The Madrona Project: Keep a Green Bough (vol. II, no. 1): "August 2020"

The Madrona Project: Human Communities in Wild Places (vol.II, no. 2): "This is Tom's poem"

Mothering (1998): "The Waning"

Pontoon (2017): "My Children Proceed"

Too Small to Hold You (Pleasure Boat Studio 2001): "Birds" and "My Mother's Nipples"

Western Journal of Medicine (November 1998): "Grand Mal"

CURVE

I

My mother's nipples

are all around me
as I, in my own bed, dream of being
a mother. The lampshades
are milk white, and every dimple
of stuccoed ceiling is a cleft of skin.

I ask for stretch marks
silver as the hairs across
my mother's brow. I want creams and oils to stroke
over my stomach as it grows.

No more
stick figures.

I want to stop bleeding
for nine cool months.
Get fat with life. Drink cartons
of milk, imagining I could put my lips
to my own breasts, if only
to remember the heat, the sound
as I swallowed all she gave me,
all I've ever owned.

after a title by Robert Hass

Honeycomb

Beyond buzz, beyond the onomatopoeia
of desire,
the strum of air
on each iridescent wing—

subtle as the whinny of a horse
in a distant field.

Layer by layer, the intricate stems of grass
that, at the right angle, could cut
you like a knife, say only
one word
when they move
in unison—

green—

with that long *e*
so long you remember the
houses of mirrors where your
own face goes on and on into—*perhaps*—
eternity

the whinny disappearing
among those
severe grasses,
the opposite of mob mentality.
Each alone
is called *blade*
sharp, sneaky, as it asks
by color to be touched.
In unison, the grass is soft

underfoot—the mob sways to the wind, relaxes—

and if there is onomatopoeia here, yes,

the word *wisp*—

of hair, of grasses—

wind lending itself   to the open field
as the flower asks
for bees
a sound joined by the thousand other bodies
wings not blades

and the hum
of desire rises
from the hive
as it rises in my own trunk—funny word
for the grace of hip and shoulder, the sway of womb
this place contains—

and the sound of the hum of desire
is not a whinny across the field, not a bee
working through the o's of the comb to create that name
appearing and reappearing through the centuries
and residing inside our lips
our taste buds
that sacred, ancient syrup—*honey*.

The trunk can do nothing
but go along for the ride, amazed
that such pleasure resides

in a single, damaged,
full-of-holes body.

Almost Talking

for Tom

In Charlotte's poem
it is a bamboo pole
single, hollow, old
that the painter traces and traces in pen and ink
until he knows its curve and tone so well
he can feel the lost leaves
almost talking.

For Alice, it's the way the cellist
leans into the wood,
into the waist and hollow
that shape him. Leans into
then away from
wind, sound, measure—
bows.

For you, my friend,
the curve of a soccer ball is
what meets the edge of our step
and is suddenly given to wind—but not this alone.

It is also the way one kick, one man, one
cannot do it alone, and the way
we can't see the space that will appear
before it is there   absolutely
the bodies ascending along cut grass, to pass,
give away, and then just as suddenly
the swoosh of goal, net bracing the hit then giving back
this simple sphere, this measure

like and unlike Bach, the up and up
of crescendo, the closing strokes,
Charlotte's painter
seeing his bamboo
after a thousand drafts
not as lines and shadow
but the space around the hollow pole
where the bones of the hands
meet the breath of the leaves
and deftly occupy open space
to find what was there all along.

For the Students Who Loved Elizabeth Bishop's "Sestina"

for Sandy McPherson

We write to remember the way words
come softly into our mouths—
to remember the way our tongues slip
through our mouths to shape each word—some primal movement,
pre–carpal tunnel. We write poems
so tears can become tea water and drop onto Bishop's almanac
and because these tears stay tears. Not only symbol but rhythm
of sestina, and math comes into it. We write because there are
stories to tell, because screams and whispers coincide,
and because this earth is a battlefield,
language the only way to bring the weapons down,
and because language is a weapon, language is music,
and because we come from places that are rooted in names,
           in kinship.

We write because music is language
and without words poetry would still live in the fingers
and bones of ancient mortar, in the lime and feldspar.
We write because *lime* and *feldspar* sound
so much like *thyme* and *larkspur*, we know
life goes on inside a worm's belly even as a bee
hums its way through the hive or a loose one buzzes
across this road
where my car might or might not crash into the small body.

We write because we coexist on the earth—near each other—
at least for a while. We write to remember Elizabeth Bishop
and Adrienne Rich and Paula Gunn Allen
and Audre Lorde and César Vallejo. We write for Vallejo
whose death came on a particular Friday and this day returns
like so many hummingbirds to sweet, clear water, to the days
when sun and rain mingle. We write because two horses met in
        a field
in Rochester, Minnesota, and this is again a blessing.
We write to describe our own horses and to hear the word
flank resound. We write because we want to say Thursday aloud
one hundred times over, to hear the tunes of blackbirds and fiddles,
to hear the click of the clogs on a young girl's feet. We write
        and write
and write while Bishop's tears become six different forms in
        one poem
and a new poem each time I see you.

The Waning

Early morning. Hungry and sucking
on small knuckles, you wake me, and through the east window
a slim moon appears in the open winter sky.

Come, child. Remind me that this moment will pass
and because I can't hold it, I'll hold you
and laugh as the moon tricks me into thinking it waxes

while you, my sweet Maeve, you grow larger, brighter
as if my arms may suddenly be
too small to hold you.

Birds

It's not so much the flight
for our baby who sees walking upright
as a kind of miracle
        but how suddenly they occupy the sky.
        Today they are seagulls, common glaucous
fishing the sound for smelt, fishing close to this ferry
that carries us from island to mainland
to island again—and if we are willing to risk the cold

our daughter
will show us the way, stretch her arms
her whole body skyward.
        Most crossings we have stayed indoors
        accustomed to the cabin, its dull heat.
But our daughter has learned to point.
Risk the wind, her gentle pull tells us,
risk the wind, and we do. We follow her
small, pointing hand into the cold

and there they are—

first one,
then a cluster, then one again,
chatter leading them
as much as their beautiful, titled wings—

our laughter sudden, abundant,
as if today were the first day
you loved me.

The curve of your foot

as my own arch finds it in the dark
doesn't tell me whether you lie
on your back or side or belly—
not yet. Only warmth
only the smooth feel of skin on even
calloused soles—or if I'm in

my socks, the fabric,
cotton or wool. And it surprises me

that I anticipate warmth or humor
or the light of morning, that even

in this perfect moment of full darkness
next to you, I long for the next moment
whether it be light or full or quiet. I long

and the length of our bodies
shares the queen bed with a toddler
now nudged between us, now jiggling
a little, not waking or
waking you. Outside
the stars do not hide. They are simply
obscured by clouds that have no agenda
but to move and rise and collect.

The curve of the sole
of your foot is beautiful
not because someday
it will be bone—
the breakable strength that shapes us—

but because tonight it is warm with the touch of skin
and the darkness
that allows us
to see.

Etiquette

How was I to know
when she said *heel*, she meant
the bread, and this, the end

              as gift?

The bread is crisp
        exact
          is warm because she baked the loaves today.
My own mother bought bread

but mostly crackers, *less fattening*, and too much
cheese wasn't good for us either. My lover chunks

dense pieces off the block of cheddar. I don't eat them.
He will follow his mother, bake bread, and be
          some part of myself I look for, some way I find
to be new in his world. I eat crackers, tasting for the crunch
for a kind of
           crust
when a *heel* was someone else,
         was someone *unkind,* in my mother's language.
And I savor these words.
            Offered the heel, I am
               unsure, awkward, and hungry.

Returning Home After the Cervical Biopsy

I pour glass after glass
of cold milk, and drink—

                    my whole mouth, throat
                    coated in layers of cream.

I drink as if the milk
were my own, so close
were the twinges of pain—

                    so sudden   unattended.

                          He had said, "Your uterus
                          may contract . . . a little"

Mine seized, with blood
racing, though all I knew
was gradual warming, the texture
of sweat rising
as I lay still
along a strip
of sterile paper sheets, so far

from orgasm, so close
to the center
of my sex.

After Insomnia

I walk among jellyfish.
Their nimble veins still
and glisten in curves of sand.

This is the time in between tides,
unsettled, and I lean close, squint
into pools of jelly and light—

the glare on the surface of clear bodies,
drying by and by. Salt winds

tickle, and I wake to the surest
sign of sleep—a circle of spittle and breath
collecting on my pillow, muses of just-waking

trembling in my limbs.

My children proceed

as if all they see is sentient:
as if the balloon
with its stretched skin breathes.

Even its descent to the floor
after days and days of lift and hover
holds meaning. And the leaves

as they scatter over frozen ground
beg Liam's question: "Where
will they sleep?"

When Maeve woke today,
she said, "I had zero dreams last night,"
meaning the nightmares, for now, are gone.

She hadn't seen
the flicker, didn't know
it fell dead on our deck,

wings spread wide,
a collection of spotted feathers
almost suggesting a bed.

Her father won't bury
the bird. His plan: to tie flies
from that scattering of feathers.

No wonder he looks
at the thousand shades
on each wing

and sees something beyond
this sudden crash, this death.
He sees a task, a fly, a piece

of the sentient world. He sees
a reflection of water, a fish rising
to catch sewn feathers believing

they are nourishment,
life, the precise light each of us
so wants to own.

Insomnia

When I walk into the yard,
bathrobe wrapped tightly around me,
a smell of earth rises like a shape, and though I cannot see
the mud, the soil, it surrounds me. More than the timothy
that wisps back and forth with what little wind there is,
more than the bees who will appear midday with their noise
and color, the buzz dazzling its way from flower to flower
preparing for spring, it is the smell that surprises.

Tonight the soles of my feet glide, accepted
by wet earth. It isn't that I want to take
my shoes off, let mud suck up and into the spaces
between each toe, only
that I like the word *mud*
more and more,
like it better than *humus* or *soil* or *dust*
and I want
to know it is there, dark and rich and right now
seeming like the opposite of insomnia—
darkness, compost, field, crickets, tree frogs, light.

This is Tom's poem,

the one he could have written
if he had just typed the words.

Instead he listened.

His mother said she could not die
because she could not get
comfortable. There was the pain—
the adjustments, the shift of pillows,
the way her feet ached, and the way
the nasal canula dried out the oxygen-rich breath
of those last days. Tom replied, "Buddhists
say let go of attachments.
What is holding you?
Shall we make a list?"

She agreed.
"The taxes need to be paid."
Tom said he would do that. "The flowers
need watering." Tom nodded, wrote that down.

Between them, simply the list.
Her words in her son's handwriting.

She trusted him, so he wrote and then put down the pencil,
took one of her feet between his hands, rubbed her heel,

sole, and the tops of her toes, reached for the other,
then lay down nearby in the second bed
in a bedroom that was once her own mother's room
when she would visit that cabin. The lake water kept lapping
on to the shore, as it had done. The stars got brighter, as they do,
and Tom was asleep
when his mother
died.

What word shall I use? What phrase?
Letting go deserves
something more than words,
more than this borrowed poem:
the list,
a gift,

a way

Curve is a word

I embrace every time,
the *u* a curve in itself, and the *c*
that leads us in, there it is,

another curve, another sense of loop,
of the circular, allowed
even in this season of pandemic fears

of isolation and distance
when both smiles and sighs
are masked,

this season when it became harder to hear
one another, harder to listen to the way the wind allows

us to notice that time loops
back on around, and the maple leaves
that were once green still carry
a paint-splash of that hue
here and there as the gold
becomes them,

and the pull
of gravity is not heavy
on these occasions after all.

The leaves float   move

through the curves

of the molecules
above the soil—

find their way, in their own time,
to the place
where they will be
humus

where mushroom abundance
might remind us

that the curve
of the earth
is too small to see,
yet defines us

allows us to breathe.

Snails and wet moss

have so many *s*'s
I remember the story
of my grandmother, the swing of her skirt,
the stitches in the hem, and the skating she did—
figure eights to impress us—right there in Central Park
just before she slipped
broke her ribs
but that was not the only time
she lost her balance.

Years later, a green bean
on the linoleum Shop Rite floor
took her down, so she needed a hip
to be stitched. Back then, the idea of replacement
absurd, they tried to just let the bones heal.

When Grandma lost her memory,
her short-term thoughts
that is,
she took on a lisp,
and maybe that is why the moss and snails
remind me to remember my grandmother, the one I knew,
the one who said the "Hail Mary" and "Our Father"
when she no longer
knew the words
of my name.

She lived in a city all those years, so I don't
have any clue whether she knew
the glory of mosses, the way feathery green becomes a kind
of carpet. And the word *carpet,* cliché as it is, tells the story
of the forest floor, the way, even now, the trees remember
what held them, what covered the home that always
would be theirs, with or without
the grace or burden
of a name.

August 2020

When is the door not a door?
When it is ajar.

I

A joke Tom used to tell returns
as I wash the lids for the jam

then boil them, while berries
sit in a colander, wait to be rinsed.

The door being ajar
is not danger, not today.

With summer fully present, a jar
becomes a kind of welcome,

an invitation to enter—and the door ajar
is a way a teen tells her mother

it is okay, maybe, to come in, but first,
please knock.

Even though the opening is here,
this entryway is also private.

II

And when the last jar
of last year's trailing blackberry jam is cracked open—

the batch that took four trips
to that small circle of trail on the DNR lands

while we waited for more to ripen,
the summer before masks were required—

our grown son is asleep upstairs, too far away
to notice the delight of this moment.

III

I am here, a mother, a woman
who was once that teenaged daughter

with her door cracked open just enough
to let in a little bit of light.

This morning I am making coffee, allowing
the dark roast to mix with a swirl of cream,

telling myself old jokes, and just briefly
noticing the possibility

that my own mother might whisper
from the other side of everything.

I let our son sleep in—remember the berries—
a year ago, ten years ago, four decades ago—

as if I might taste the rain, the sun,
alongside the bitter seeds,

and dip my spoon into the open jar.

Neowise

Above our home, the forest opens to meadow.
Beyond this, across the lane and to the north,
a For Sale sign, slightly bleached by sun.

The place was cleared for timber
or for the view. Either way, a clearcut
is not what the earth needs,

plus the neighbors heard
two bears scrounging around their compost
then saw them tipping garbage bins, cruising the easement roads

just after dark—or whenever they liked. Tonight
we walk into that clearcut, grateful for the sunset,
for physical distance, lay wool blankets down

on the stubble of grasses, allow darkness to fold into night.
When stars appear, we rely on binoculars, hoping to catch a
glimpse of Neowise, the comet everyone keeps
mentioning,

the one you need to see now
or wait something like seven thousand years
for another viewing, which just this afternoon

caused Waverly to ask,

"Do you think people
will still be here on earth then?"

A breeze sweeps up from the north side
of Lost Mountain, and the air feels brisk,
the colors changing, the trees almost two-dimensional.

For a moment I forget the meaning
of a year, allow time and distance, anticipation, fear
to be held

and let go. I breathe in
this simple, cool breeze arriving
just past sunset.

Creaky hinges

are a sign of insomnia,
a prompt, perhaps,
a way to find
the direction of
no sleep
and so many *no* phrases
so many ways
to feel the body resist. *Hinge*
has flow, has a way of moving
into itself—the *g* particularly curly, right here,
pronouncing *Grrrr* and *Gee* and thus, *Gee whiz...*

Is this the growl of tiger, of fear
followed by the lighthearted, goofy
phrase from some childhood I never fully knew?

Creaky hinges are not a horror story. They are
the house continuing to become itself
whether or not
a pandemic rages
and no matter what the news says,
delivered on the small
rectangular screen
of an iPhone.

Regardless, the house settles.
What I wish for is the kind
of sleep that brings good dreams,
deep and vivid,

but also ones with
more of a *gee whiz*
lightness to them.

Either way, they allow my body
to hinge itself into the place
where I feel most safe and sound
where the sounds of the home I inhabit
may include creaky bones
and also the subtle music
of a way
not so much forward
but simply into
the curve
of the syllable
of now.

March 20, 2020

for Mary

A chilly overcast in the Pacific Northwest

but signs of spring
find me anyway, as I turn the dial
on my old-school radio
in the car my father owned
when he died
a decade ago, thinking
anything but the news . . .

I turn south onto 7th, toward the Safeway
parking lot,
and there they are:
a path of cherry trees, blossoming
along each side of this paved road
and the word *border*
disappears—

Those light blossoms
remind me of one year ago, when I drove
to UW Medical Center because the bleeding
might mean
something.

I drove to Seattle, the place
that saw our first cases of COVID 19,
and our daughter waited for me
in a room painted white

then walked me to the center
of campus, to a small orchard

where petals floated in the blue easiness of sky—

The wind picked up, and we walked
toward the twisted gray trunks—
So many flowers
drifted down

we began to see the blossoms
as snowfall, and I thought maybe I could
drop right there, right then,
shape an angel in the petals.

We stood in the orchard while the pink flakes,
the certain blossoms
covered us
made us remember
everything
except the reason we came here

to begin with.

I never knew I'd miss

my father's phone calls. Never realized
they were a kind
of solace
I recognize now

as the familiar soil
of mourning—a kind
of earth darkness
that keeps skunk cabbage
and calypso orchids
returning
and when

I reached the bridge on the Elwha,
I saw the place where water
is a blue
remembered,
a depth in the river

so vivid I wanted to say
those two syllables aloud:
Merced   the place in the heart
of Yosemite my father returned
each year   *with us, for us,*
so we could have the thrill
of leaping off that bridge,
letting our bodies

fall
fully
into the river.

Tonight, this memory of the Merced is more
than mourning, more than arriving
on the side of a country road
so my husband and daughter
can find Mercury
setting
just minutes after the sun.

"It is rare to see that particular planet,"
Tom says, "no matter how close it is."
Maeve adds, "Galileo never even caught a glimpse.
But here we are."

This search for the planet
brings me back to the river, as I lift
binoculars to my eyes and see less of the sky
as I focus. A light overcast hovers
at the horizon, and I search on behalf of my daughter
but find only Venus, then cloud patterns,
track those for a while, then lower the Nikons
to dangle near my heart
on a thin nylon rope that keeps me
from misplacing them.
We stand shoulder to shoulder, Mercury eluding us
as any trickster might do, and my father's presence returns, peculiar
and stunning as a constellation I never expected to find.

Grand Mal

I'd rather say it was cold that morning,
earth frozen hard, a scuff of frost on the outside glass.

I'd rather write of the sky, less
like fur or hair than granite. I'd rather

speak of anything defined or distant
than to remember the sound of his choked

scream coming from the downstairs bathroom.
That my mother did scream released me—

"Your father... hurry," her body a blur—
and I remember the door opening

as he lashed, fought, then fell, silent—
toes curled under, fingers entwined

only to each other, eyes rolling back
just far enough not to know us. I tell you:

It wasn't cold. I was in shorts, and his head lay heavy
against my thigh, his lips dry between hard breaths

as I turned his face slowly to find some position
even suggesting rest. A bird called out, surely

a robin—sound lifting through screened windows
across this muddy, lighted season. I listened

for my father, and not a word came from his open mouth—
tongue held tight in Mother's hand.

"Not much for small talk,"

said the famous poet,
riding in the front seat of the car
tripping his fingers across the keys
on his iPhone. In the driver's seat

a student, the one who offered
to chauffeur this writer she so admired,
sat silent, and that is the end of the story.
The quiet movement of turning the blinker on,

the disappointment or perhaps rage.
Today, the phrase returns to me, *small talk,*
as I sift through letters and newspaper clippings in the attic
realizing that this too is a kind of conversation.

Small notes, handwritten cards, even
a pad of yellow-lined paper my mother
kept on her desk. In the midst of these cursive letters
and the typed correspondence, I think

of Charlotte, who said she'd felt bereft
after leaving her husband's clothes at Serenity House,
not the moment when she handed the boxes over,
not the moment she drove away from the brick building,

but later, at home, when she suddenly wondered
how her skirts and blouses might get along
without George's jackets and slacks
and especially the long sleeves of his seersucker shirts.

The clothes over fifty-eight years
of their marriage having that conversation
was beautiful, was their life itself,
and as I think of the phrase,

I wonder what else is between us
but the precious connections of small talk,
the everyday touch, sleeve to sleeve,
help with the clasp of a necklace.

And if we are blessed
to pay attention to each other's questions,
each other's answers over time,
"Have you been to the Skagit Valley?"

opens into the ecology
of tulips and black bears,
salmon circling and finding their way
upstream, and the missed opportunity

of small exchanges, of languages
we have not yet come to know.
May that student who was dismissed by the famous poet
change her story—may she have noticed

the particular light on the edges of the highway
on this rural, familiar road as she passed the abundance
of tulips not yet blossomed. I hope she turned to listen
instead to her own heart beating, the small talk

of her life guiding her, even then, through a place
she loves. And may the words she found
be the beginning of her own next poem
as she remembers the way

the small moments, the talk, or the silence
can carry us into a light more abundant
for this imperfect language
we share.

On the Trail to the First Bald, Deer Ridge, May 2020

If they whisper to you,
the tiny, almost imperceptible curves of air

on the wind,
if they begin to suggest
that the rhododendron petals
are about to disperse, are heading, as they always do,
to the soil,
if they say
"I apologize for the laughter
in the shadows;
it is not meant to hurt you,"

perhaps you will find, even amid
trepidation, that this day
is ok. Is enough.

Realize those aren't dangerous voices you hear.
Just the sounds of change, and indeed

the rhododendrons are brightest
when their buds are fisted up.
They are not violence, not angst—
simply promise.
When they open, color becomes
a window to light, and bees find their way home,

nourished and abundant in the buzz and shimmer
of this very afternoon.

III

After the Hysterectomy

When a poet friend wrote that
she had *mined* her journal
for poems, I cringed. *Mine* as verb

no longer possible
after the hysterectomy.

Words shifted meaning—
metamorphic rock, sediment
depending.

Change sudden
as cell division, quick as a knife
through skin
that holds a body together.

Not long ago, I had
welcomed *mine* into the vocabulary
of finding treasures
of what was—

And what about *time*—

the tone when accused,
by Father, mostly of wasting it—

and it turns out

killing time
allows no room for being
in the presence
of what is.

That is mine rings
with a playground pitch
of stripping the air
of sound
while hands grab
an object.

When does *hyster*
become womb again,
when might this *hiss*
lose the connection with Freud's indictment,

the illness only women can own?
When my uterus was taken

this was
a necessary violence—

the risk of endometrial cancer
dismissed, possibly even
erased.

The stillness continues
to settle. A space inside me, a fist-sized

organ, once a home, now gone.
Might as well have been a planet.

I say *womb* aloud
once in a while, just
for good measure.

After a Line by Chief Dan George

for Dr. Christine Blasey Ford

Keep a few embers from the fire,
whether they are the glow of a hearth
remaining
or the last of what was used
to burn your village
down—
keep a few.

The hot coals are not
poison
but promise,
and the way the night sky
seems terribly
terrifyingly
dark
can be a kind of path, be a way
to seeing
the undercurrent
of every color in that black expanse.
Stars or no stars,
cloud cover or rain, this body is your home.

If the coals are dark, shift
your rake

into the darkness,
move the teeth of the metal
side to side, tend the heat.
Because of your hand in this, the power
will be
unsettled.
Exhale into the darkness. Your breath will lift
the coal into gold, into the color of beginnings.
Only such close tending
will entice the pile to full red,
sanguine, deep-pain light.

Now include the wood.
Not fresh logs but aging or aged
sticks and roots,
maybe even a stump lifted by a larger tool—
a bull-dozer will do.

Take that.

Keep moving into the pain of unsettling.
Necessary light will arrive. Will warm you.
Hands first.
Rub them, entwine them,
move them into and through each other.
Warmth will find its way
back home.

Remember to speak into the growing flames.
You are not alone.

A Tale Disappearing

Shadows get a bad rap.
I notice they stretch ahead of me, lengthening
my stature, strengthening my resolve,
giving the appearance
that this body can transform,
this body can tower
over
                across
                                  through
borders.
Shadow as underdog is a tale disappearing.

At night, shadows overtake.

That black expanse of sky

allows a moon

to expand us.

I walk my rescue pup
down a familiar path, and we grow
in the light of the moon,
we seem to rise
to lift

and I
put a spring in my step
a possible gesture
of what comes next.

Suddenly I am amazed
at what this single
body—
because we have survived—
can do.

I see us all
stepping
together
and just how light
our power appears
in so much darkness.

IV

March 11

When I saw the waves on the ocean that morning,
my whole body
shimmered awake.
No one told me my skin would lift
to feel the air
she no longer knew,
the boards above the sand holding me,
holding the weight of this day,
still only seven in the morning.

When she passed away, daylight savings
had just sprung forward. Four a.m.,
and most of the town was still asleep,
their alarms set for church at dawn,
keeping track of the hour
they'd lost overnight.

No cherry blossoms this morning, no signs
of spring. Only the weatherman saying
snow had been predicted,
saying, *This sun is a real surprise, quite something.*

In that moment on the boardwalk
waves shimmered, my skin rose to meet
their light, and I could have sworn
my mother's laughter lifted into wind.

In the living room, the hospital bed lay empty.
We never lit the fire our mother wanted,
for fear the oxygen tank was too close,
and besides, there was so little time.
As I walked out that door, half past six a.m.,
the black-suited funeral-home guys
having taken her body with them,
there was only emptiness.

I walked until I could see the early-morning surfers silhouetted
in their own black suits, as the waves carried them to shore.

I walked and walked
until those same waves shimmered
into air, and continued on the boardwalk that had held up
for more than two hundred years,
that held up for me
this body of light.

Adopting a Lovebird in Autumn

I

Last night, I dreamt my mother had a few weeks left
and in the familiar scape of dreaming,

I drew near her on the plush front seat
of the old car—she truly was
still alive—though when I reached to her face
nothing held me, no warm cheek met my cupped palm—

II

No wonder the lovebird's touch,
his head nuzzling under my open hand and in between
each finger, is a salve—no wonder the wings feel familiar
and distant at once,
clipped before they realized
their limits—
and the shade of blue
deep in the tail feathers
surprising me
among all that green, that silky body,
all that color
at daybreak or nightfall, or this right-now
autumn morning in my own home—

where a tiny bird simply wants me to reach out

to where skin meets feathers and no one is thinking
about the cage.
The wings like a dream unfinished
but fluttering all the same.

Grief

Making blackberry jam—
the splash of the spoon carries thick, round berries
into a liquid that changes color
with heat. She sees the sun
has pierced through overcast skies. She wants
to remember how sun ripens the fruit, changes
the depth of flavor. But the weight of 2007
returns—not a cloud, not a metaphor—
the year her mother died.

Fruit ripens, even in rain. Sun is carried
across open fields as soon as clouds part, even briefly.
On the phone, her brother tells her
it is unusually warm in New Jersey:
"The ocean is great.
We were riding waves today."
And she pictures him howling
as he dives under and through the salt water,
tosses back his hair and goes at it again.

Nearly forty-five years old, he still looks like a teen,
as if they were in some other story,
some other more likely picture,
where their mother is alive,
worrying he'll catch cold,
hoping for the best.

Autumn 2007, her brother dives into waves—
the rush of what we can't predict
a kind of hope.

Three thousand miles away, stirring
the thick boil of juice, she wants to be grateful,
not simply for the sun
divided day by day then held in the small circles
of each black sphere and in the berry's center.
She wants to see these afternoons, drinking tea as her mother
                    would have,
a kind of ripening. She pictures her brother

tossing back his hair, swimming into the next wave,
and though her mother never
rode those swells, her spirit rises,
sure and inconceivable
as the taste of blackberries, the reticence of grace.

Morse Creek Turning

after Raymond Carver

I picked up a maple leaf
only partially changed. Right side
lit with yellow, left still holding faded
green. Veins were etched in a pattern
of in-betweens, gold and yellow, maroon and green, suggesting

topographical maps, pages to read near the side of a river,
midsummer, watching a dipper bob in and out
of currents. Drawn in by this not-yet-finished
story, by this sign of autumn and the coming cold; drawn in by
                a leaf
pulled down too soon, before the full shimmer of gold, full
                stacatto
of leaf on stem on leaf came to pass,

I leaned down, taking the long stem
between two fingers, only solid as river rocks,
shaped by the whims of the day.

This morning, light
ripples through
the still surface of the Strait,
seeps into the maze
of kelp below. Last time I walked this trail someone said,
"There is so much gunk in the water,

it looks dirty," pointing
to the habitat below,
the mysterious home of sea lion,
otter, and coho.

How little we know. How many thousand
molecules does it take for a single wave to form on a single
creek? This fine autumn morning, I pick up as many leaves
as I like, twirl them by the stem. The in-between is all we have.

When the ferry horn bellows,
telling me that fog may roll in, changing
the whole shape of this day,
I feel the baritone in ripples, in shimmers across my skin.

The kelp forests listen,
and the sun moves a notch higher
in the sea-blue sky.

Grief II

Blackberries boiling on the stovetop
are not violence. Their color changes.
Jam scent lifts into air
long before we can taste
the transformation, long before
it cools and thickens, becomes what we
remember of last summer's heat.

Making the jam is simply a task,
while autumn lights the leaves with that certain
slant of color—perhaps the opposite of hope—
and my husband tells me
it's the sugar in the leaves
that makes them change, tells me
even though there has been a warm spell in New Jersey,
land of my mother's death, still
the leaves will pass.

The jam is no longer the color of berries.
Sugar has transformed
this small task. The jars sit
unassuming
on the counter.

In fifteen minutes
they'll begin to seal themselves.
Even as we busy our lives into the next moment,

lift the dustpan to the trash bin or sip tea in the waning light,
the sound of the jars surprises us, the click of it
(tongue on roof of mouth)
makes us turn and look, though
we knew all along
our stirring, our patience,

our task completed,
was just
the beginning.

St. Placid Priory

When the cup is half-empty
I am not even thirsty,
stomach as hollow as a
field of wheat shorn
lower than the wind.
No breeze. No rain. Not even silence. When it is half
empty, I hate the expression. But oh, how
the midline accepts its pleasure.

The cup fills up
while you walk into the woods, the hollows,
even a field of scotchbroom—and sneeze
until your eyes blur and your ears can't hear. Only notice
the rhododendron that share this slope
with noxious weeds. Only hope your roots
though fragile here
just two weeks after your mother's passing
will hold. Only hope that what is indistinguishable
midwinter, green to green,
while needles turn to mulch underfoot,
will bloom
and drops of rain fill
not the imagined glass but the palms
of the rhododendron leaves
even before we notice.

Grief III

The blackberry jam
not yet made
is a story of summer
gone cold. Too many clouds
for the juniper bushes to bud, the apple petals to fill
the valleys, as if my mother's passing
slowed the process, kept the blossoms hidden, as if what matters
and does not matter is the juice of the berries, how sweet it
                        tastes

on fingers, on bread, on whatever will accept its promise.
When I stand at my kitchen stove,
stir the ripe berries into a boil, the wooden spoon is stained
with last year's berries and the year before's and the one
before that. I go to the work, to the jam berries
to keep them from molding, to try to stop time.

Come December I will wrap the jars, drop them in the heel
of stockings.
               Christmas morning, the fruit will remind me
of everything
except loss.

In the Dark

The blackberry farm
down the end of Windy Way
is open *even at midnight*, so my seven-year-old
tells me. It is October. Leaves still cling
to the brittle stems of maple, alder.
Fion explains that we can
take flashlights, find ripe berries in the dark.

We get ready for bed, carry stories
into the half-light of his room. The stars appear
through closed windows, budding like the apple petals
of May, like the early rhododendron I noticed just after
my mother's funeral, when the cherry trees,
full of their pink announcements, must have given
some neighbors cause to smile. No flashlights needed.
No extra batteries. The days themselves were growing longer.
My mother loved each sign of spring, from the cliché of green
to the hidden scent of magnolia; loved when the clocks sprung
                    forward.

Once I picked a bouquet of daisies and gardenias
from Mrs. Petrisko's garden. Didn't know I'd get in trouble.

My mother secretly treasured that gift, kept the flowers
in a vase just below the window, out of the neighbors' view.
My son, now tucked beneath the covers, begins to breathe that
                    regular

breath we long for, the simple pleasure
of falling asleep, and I want to step into the night
full of spiders and ripe fruit, want to feel
the juice of the blackberries slipping
into the creases of my fingers.

The berry is part sun, part cloud, part dust
of the Windy Way turnaround, is the story of a year, a long
exhaling breath, even when darkness may seem
to obscure the view. I want to thank
the farmer who offers us this delight
of berries at midnight, but I stay with my son,
watch him sleep,
then take the flashlight, put it in the top drawer.

Outside, the stars look
as if I could pluck one
secretly from the sky.

Maple leaf,

smaller than my palm, you might
disappear with the simplest
lift of wind, so I hold you closer,
stem between two fingers,
                              notice
the small crack that jaggedly interrupts
your topography. My own hand carries lines that someone
might read: *love* and *life*
and the single question, *How long?*
Snails make their way across the mud, followed by
trails no wider than the scrolls of time
on my hand. Will someone measure the distance?
Not today, anyway, while the cloudless sky
is so wide we need another name for *blue*
and the light shimmers so convincingly
on the small patterns of still water
in the mudflats even the oil refineries seem a mirage.

Our human hands can hold
a leaf, a pen, a vase; may lift
a child to a chair, a book to a shelf;
reach out to a stranger
in a gesture so confirming
the word *shake*
seems absurd.
Just a month ago, I held my hand out

to more than a hundred kin and neighbors who brought
condolences to my father's midafternoon wake.

"I am sorry for your loss," they said, so many o's in that phrase,
yet spoken so briskly, quietly, leaving little room
for the open circle of breath so often possible
between us. The conversations in that dimly lit
room jittered and skipped like killdeer
darting away then back to the shoreline.
Here on the mudflats this late-summer morning,
the wind picks up, and instead of taking you from my hand
like the small bird you might become
in another story, a child's tale, my fingers hold tighter,
just to keep you here,

while the brush of cool air on skin makes me raise my palm
to meet it, this breeze so intimate that I see these creases,
line to line, are watersheds, tiny as a fallen vine-maple leaf,
long and complex as the geomorphology of a river.

If my father were here, he would not notice the snails,
with their million-fold patterns of mud-born calligraphy,
choosing instead to set his eyes on the upward reach,
that unnameable color of sky
where the heron and red-tailed and falcon leave a trail
only discerned by the wind.

V

The word *evening*

is a three-syllable
story of balance.
The windows in December
allow last bits of daylight
into a kitchen warmed by the woodstove
and the simmer of stew.

This time of year, nightfall comes
abruptly, reminds me of the spring Maeve
feared evening, the time of day when light
left our small backyard.

In a tiny, two-bedroom home in Vermont,
Maeve worried, watched the edges of birch trees
in the distance becoming silhouettes, and I saw
her eyes emptying out. "Tomorrow is another
day," I would tell her, repeating my own mother's mantra,
but tomorrow was a mere concept,

not warmth, not cloud shadows on the patterned bark
of the birches or the rippling protection
of sugar maples, their leaves abundant, trunks
solid when we swung on branches sometimes
after lunch.

In the last possible minutes of sunset,
her hand reaching up to mine, she would urge, "Let's go
outside," and we would, almost every evening,

while her brother
built towers out of giant blocks
and knocked them over, laughing
then asking his daddy for more.

Outside, in the clear New England air, I knew
Orion and Cassiopeia were not far off, though their stories
always elude me, disappear, no matter
how I try to memorize. So I began
to tell Maeve about the time
we took twenty students
to the Pacific Coast.

"Low tide was at 6 o'clock in the morning," I tell her,
"so we left campus in two small buses, 3 a.m.,
just to get to Rialto in time for the tidepools."

Even the inbetween tides will hide
the urchins and sea-stars, the limpets,
crabs, and tiny mollusks.

"We woke in the dark, followed the highway
long past the Elwha River and around Lake Crescent,
down the LaPush Road, and on past Three Rivers Campsite
to the mouth of Quillayute, and climbed across
rocks and sand from the parking lot to the beach,

when suddenly one of the students stopped and called out,
pointing to pools of shallow saltwater, 'Look!'
and there it was: the night sky
reflected in the water below us."

As I tell Maeve each detail
of the story, I lose myself in the past tense of it all, not knowing
exactly why I am telling her, or why,
tonight, twenty years later,

as darkness enters our kitchen in Sequim, I tell myself
how Maeve and I held hands that night in Vermont,
found the way back to the door of our small,
shingled home, commenting to each other
that now the rooms were lit from inside.
We could hear Tom and Liam laughing
at what had fallen apart.

Whether they built that tower again
or simply sat among the blocks
in the lamplight, Maeve would do her best
to repeat the story, to tell about
the morning on Rialto Beach
when Mommy's students saw puddles
carrying the stars.

Solstice

for Tom

There are the moments
when silence

is all we need
when the candlelight

does not remind us
of anything

we've done
or not done.

And sometimes
conversation

the return
to worn chairs, our own home,

sitting together
two glasses of wine

and just a scent of the grapes
that were whole and ripe,

only this borrowed taste now
ours, the words between us

loose and abundant as stars.

First snows

cover all we didn't finish:
a path of pebbles to a makeshift dollhouse
in the woods, a pile of kindling
we meant to stash last night.

First snows get us working
on holiday cards, carving potato
stamps with Yellow Finns.
First snows tell tales:

a raccoon looking for scraps
near the compost, the spread
of owl wings and sudden
disappearance of rabbit tracks.

First snows
have us peering out windows,
checking how the white hat grows
on the aging jack-o'-lantern.

First snows tempt us. We run outside,
as if time were a gift, and the word
present a simple taste caught
on our waiting, misting tongues.

The Workshop

for Charlotte

In her poem
the blue-and-white bowl
holds oranges. Nothing else.

From the dark-wood table, her colors
rise like new light
on holy rivers.

We study the poem,
move pencils across type.
This house allows silence.

Through screens, the birds hear us hearing them
and the light step of doe surprises wet grass.

The oranges in the poem are sectioned,
precise. The rivers, though strewn with trash,
remain holy. They change course, rise and flow
from dark palms of cobbled earth.

Salmon swim against the current, their scales
rise above the blue and white
of wave and shallow.

A rufus hummingbird, silent but for the hum
of wing and hunger, watches us through the glass.

We are changed by his wings, by reflection, silence,
the memory of rivers

and a blue-and white-bowl
made holy
by what it bears.

Another March 11

My mother loved a bit
of the bubbly, especially Dom Perignon,
and I am thinking of mimosas,

the way they sparkle,
because breakfast
is a crazy time to imbibe.

I want to hear the pop of the cork,
not celebration, not that—it's just
that there is something about those bubbles,

tiny planets, perhaps,
or molecules not yet formed.
Fourteen years ago this morning, my mother died,

took her last breath just hours before sunrise.
The room held her—nothing like champagne—
more a quiet and abundant love

more a precursor to the avalanche of grief
the immensity undoing everything,
then a glimpse of the shape of this world without her.

In the hours after the funeral-home guys in their black suits
took my mother's body from us, there was a way about the room
a kind of distance and presence all at once, and I remember

the air, the shimmer of the way everything had changed
and yet even the leaves on the jade plant
and the stain of old smoke above the fireplace

were as familiar as the anticipation of opening champagne,
of pouring the first glass into a space that would hold,
just briefly, this immense potential for light.

Practice

(when my landlady knocks and I don't answer)

What I am doing is not yoga
exactly—it is the slight curve of waist
as it slips into one of the poses—

needing breath
to pronounce
what is and is not
a pose but the body itself
becoming *lion*   *mountain*   *half-moon*

the willingness to space each foot apart
so precisely, so directly, the weight

becomes equal   half into toes, half into heels, each
           spreading
into the middle of the soles

learning that the limbs, too, must breathe
that the air we inhale stretches itself
into the poses of our daily steps so we must

follow, with air and intention, until we stop answering tele-
           phones
stop knocking on doors, stop needing the word
meditation, and simply breathe the world
into our noses, our legs,

the smallest stretch
of toenail   in the room.

Wisdom, Logic, Light

for Elizabeth

There is the light,
golden as it filters
through leaves

above the river current rising
with spring runoff, a glint from nearby rocks
almost suggesting snow.

There is the softening, when the roar
slows to a hush, then the whisper, iridescent leaves
bristling as if to discuss some goings on,

and also the lulls. There is the fog, so thick we see deer
only because they graze close to the windows,
moving slowly, shoring up food for winter—

no hurry, as if this fog could shield us from anything,
as if those lithe bodies were immune to the change,
our calendars crossing over to October.

A buck so young it is hard to see the budding antlers
lulls about, close to the willow branches, and I am
glad for the fog, for the brief cover, though I know the logic of
        the hunt.

Turning the knob on the front door
minutely, so as not to startle anyone,
I listen for the gossip of leaves,

the promise of this moment,
deer grazing for as long as they like
in the filtered light of morning.

About the Author

Kate Reavey completed an MA in poetry with Gary Snyder as her mentor. She worked as a fire dispatch and interpretive ranger before deciding on a path of teaching, which she has followed for more than thirty years. Her chapbooks *Through the East-Window* (Sagittarius Press) and *Trading Posts* (Tangram) are limited-edition, letter-pressed works, and *Too Small to Hold You* was published by Pleasure Boat Studio. She coordinates Studium Generale at Peninsula College, and for many years was codirector of the Foothills Writers Series. In 2010, she taught creative writing and literature in Florence, Italy, and from 2014–18 she taught in ʔaʔkʷustəŋáwtxʷ House of Learning, Peninsula College Longhouse, for the Native Pathways Program through The Evergreen State College. Her PhD in Interdisciplinary Humanities is centered on poetry, somebodyness, and beloved community.

Poems are set in Sabon, with titles in Gill Sans.

www.emptybowl.org

CPSIA information can be obtained
at www.ICGtesting.com
Printed in the USA
BVHW081919051022
648679BV00003B/19

9 781737 040880